AUDUBON

Wild Bird Desk Diary 1995

JANUARY
S	M	T	W	T	F	S
1	2	3	4	5	6	7
8	9	10	11	12	13	14
15	16	17	18	19	20	21
22	23	24	25	26	27	28
29	30	31				

FEBRUARY
S	M	T	W	T	F	S
			1	2	3	4
5	6	7	8	9	10	11
12	13	14	15	16	17	18
19	20	21	22	23	24	25
26	27	28				

MARCH
S	M	T	W	T	F	S
			1	2	3	4
5	6	7	8	9	10	11
12	13	14	15	16	17	18
19	20	21	22	23	24	25
26	27	28	29	30	31	

APRIL
S	M	T	W	T	F	S
						1
2	3	4	5	6	7	8
9	10	11	12	13	14	15
16	17	18	19	20	21	22
23	24	25	26	27	28	29
30						

MAY
S	M	T	W	T	F	S
	1	2	3	4	5	6
7	8	9	10	11	12	13
14	15	16	17	18	19	20
21	22	23	24	25	26	27
28	29	30	31			

JUNE
S	M	T	W	T	F	S
				1	2	3
4	5	6	7	8	9	10
11	12	13	14	15	16	17
18	19	20	21	22	23	24
25	26	27	28	29	30	

JULY
S	M	T	W	T	F	S
						1
2	3	4	5	6	7	8
9	10	11	12	13	14	15
16	17	18	19	20	21	22
23	24	25	26	27	28	29
30	31					

AUGUST
S	M	T	W	T	F	S
		1	2	3	4	5
6	7	8	9	10	11	12
13	14	15	16	17	18	19
20	21	22	23	24	25	26
27	28	29	30	31		

SEPTEMBER
S	M	T	W	T	F	S
					1	2
3	4	5	6	7	8	9
10	11	12	13	14	15	16
17	18	19	20	21	22	23
24	25	26	27	28	29	30

OCTOBER
S	M	T	W	T	F	S
1	2	3	4	5	6	7
8	9	10	11	12	13	14
15	16	17	18	19	20	21
22	23	24	25	26	27	28
29	30	31				

NOVEMBER
S	M	T	W	T	F	S
			1	2	3	4
5	6	7	8	9	10	11
12	13	14	15	16	17	18
19	20	21	22	23	24	25
26	27	28	29	30		

DECEMBER
S	M	T	W	T	F	S
					1	2
3	4	5	6	7	8	9
10	11	12	13	14	15	16
17	18	19	20	21	22	23
24	25	26	27	28	29	30
31						

Bald eagle (*Haliaeetus leucocephalus*). Chilkat River, Alaska. Nikon F4 with 300mm lens, Fujichrome Velvia. By Daniel J. Cox.

AUDUBON

Wild Bird Desk Diary 1995

MACMILLAN PUBLISHING COMPANY   *New York*

MAXWELL MACMILLAN CANADA   *Toronto*

MAXWELL MACMILLAN INTERNATIONAL
New York   Oxford   Singapore   Sydney

Purple finch (*Carpodacus purpureus*) on red-osier dogwood (*Cornus stolonifera*). Near Brainerd, Minnesota. Nikon F4 with 400mm lens, Fujichrome Velvia at 1/125 second/F8. By Bill Marchel.

Photo editing by Monica B. Lamontagne. Creative supervision by Wendy G. Batteau. Text by Stephen W. Kress, Ph.D. Design by Janet Tingey. Production editing by Andrew Attaway. Display lettering by Julian Waters.

Jewish holidays begin at sunset on the previous evening. Astronomical information is given in Eastern Standard Time and Eastern Daylight Time (when applicable). Eclipses noted are visible from the Americas.

ISBN 0-02-079948-9

*Front Cover: Female American kestrel (*Falco sparverius*) sitting in sugar maple tree (*Acer saccharum*). Nikon F4 with 500mm lens and TC 14B converter, Fujichrome Velvia at 1/125 second/F5.6 . By Rich Kirchner.*

Wild Birds Are in Jeopardy

PAUL R. EHRLICH

PEOPLE WHO build model airplanes face no shortage of kits; stamp collectors are not about to run out of stamps to squirrel away; sports fans have a seemingly endless array of events to watch; gardeners won't run out of seeds; music lovers can immerse themselves in the clear sounds of compact disks. These and other hobbyists face no obvious threats to the pursuit of their avocation or, for that matter, to their children pursuing it. Not so birders. There are many fewer migrant songbirds in eastern forests these days; ducks are dramatically down in numbers; shorebirds appear to be in decline also.

This decline can be traced directly to habitat alteration and outright destruction by humanity. In the Southeast, most of the swamps in which wood storks once foraged have been drained to free land for growing crops or building homes or factories. Similarly, most of the extensive bottomland cypress forests that ivory-billed woodpeckers divided up into breeding territories (of up to two thousand acres) have been destroyed and the birds extirpated from the United States. Bachman's warbler is presumed to have suffered both from the clearing of extensive canebrake breeding habitat to make room for crops and from a loss of habitat in its Caribbean wintering grounds. In coastal Texas and Louisiana the open prairies required by Attwater's greater prairie-chicken have all but disappeared under farm fields, homes, and oil-drilling operations. In the West, decimation of riparian zone vegetation by cattle grazing is behind willow flycatcher declines.

In other cases, changes in habitats are more subtle. Eastern screech owls have suffered from the creosote preservative applied to telephone poles, which reduces the survival of young in nest cavities in the poles. The red-cockaded woodpecker and purple martin are jeopardized by forestry practices that harvest trees before they are mature and suitable for nesting, and that eliminate standing dead trees. Land-use changes, in particular the replacement of forests with farms, have promoted the increase and spread of that efficient brood parasite, the brown-headed cowbird, which has reduced populations of many songbird species. Cowbird control is now employed to help keep Kirtland's warbler and the black-capped vireo from disappearing altogether.

Invasions of exotic organisms are a type of habitat modification that has had serious impacts on many bird populations. Hairy woodpeckers, red-headed woodpeckers, and eastern and western bluebirds all seem to be suffering from competition for nest-holes from imported house sparrows and European starlings. Predation by arctic foxes introduced to the Aleutian Islands was a prime factor in the decline of the Aleutian Canada goose.

Extensive efforts are underway to preserve some of our most imperiled birds. Many are based on the Endangered Species Act (ESA), a landmark piece of legislation, but one that nonetheless is sadly deficient. The ESA draws attention to species or subspecies only after their declines are well advanced, instead of focusing on maintaining widespread, healthy, natural ecosystems that can support both wildlife and a healthy human society. Environmental scientists have tried to use the ESA to preserve ecosystems, but their efforts often are misunderstood. The northern spotted owl, for instance, helps *protect* the remaining northwestern old-growth forest that is essential to the long-term health of the timber industry. The ESA needs to be made a better vehicle for keeping vital services that ecosystems provide to society from faltering further.

But I fear the ESA will be weakened, not strengthened. In the long run, perhaps even within the next couple of decades, many of our efforts to save imperiled birds seem destined to fail. As the U.S. population (now third largest in the world) approaches 300 million, as habitat destruction in Latin American wintering grounds accelerates, and as the scale of the global human enterprise grows, the problems confronting birds will grow apace. "Human needs" will increasingly be cited as the reason for destroying additional critical habitat.

But human needs and those of our dwindling avifauna are actually congruent. Global warming, ozone depletion, wetland destruction, desertification, and urbanization of land threaten not only the birds, but civilization itself. For instance, climate change that would exterminate Kirtland's warbler also could substantially reduce U.S. agricultural productivity.

So if you care whether our grandchildren will enjoy a fine diversity of birds to watch for fun (or, indeed, if they'll have a decent world to live in), become an environmental activist. Birding is fun, but joining an organization dedicated to preserving a livable planet and working with like-minded people has its pleasures, too. Think about it as you enjoy the beautiful birds in this diary. Becoming active in the Audubon Society, if you are not already, would be a good place to start.

Paul R. Ehrlich is Bing Professor of Population Studies at Stanford University, and co-author of The Birder's Handbook *and* Birds in Jeopardy.

Male American goldfinch (*Carduelis tristis*). Near Ithaca, New York. Nikon FE2 with 400mm EDIF lens, Fujichrome Velvia at 1/60 second/F4. By Marie Read.

Tree-Clinging Birds

WHILE MOST forest birds migrate to warmer climates during winter, tree-clinging birds such as woodpeckers, nuthatches, and creepers remain. These birds glean insects, spiders, and other sleeping invertebrates from the crevices and cracks in trees, finding ample food to weather the most severe winters.

Each of the tree-clinging birds picks or excavates food from the tree trunk either in a different way or from a slightly different place—in this way they each find ample food reserves. Woodpeckers inspect the tree trunk from an upright perspective, while nuthatches examine the same bark while hanging upside down. Tiny brown creepers start foraging at the base of a tree and spiral their way upward, hitching themselves along like woodpeckers. Unlike woodpeckers, which have straight, chisel-like beaks, brown creepers have thin, downward curved beaks which they use to extract sleeping insects, pupae, and eggs from tree bark, much as we might use a curved finger to extract a hidden coin from a tight-fitting car seat.

Woodpeckers range in size from the sparrow-sized downy woodpecker to the crow-sized pileated woodpecker. There are about two hundred species of woodpeckers worldwide—twenty-three of these occur in North America. Most woodpeckers are sedentary because their lives are centered on tree trunks. Their feet are wonderfully adapted for clinging to bark, with two toes facing up and two facing back for better balance. All species have a stiff tail, which serves as a rigid prop.

Although woodpeckers usually excavate their own nesting and roosting cavities, not all species feed on tree trunks. Some woodpeckers, such as the red-headed woodpecker of eastern North America, rarely drill trees. Instead, they often perch atop dead snags and fly out to capture insect prey from midair like flycatchers. They balance their diet by feeding on acorns, beechnuts, and grains. Flickers, another group of unorthodox woodpeckers, feed mainly on the ground, where they probe for ants.

Since flying insects are scarce during winter months and the ground is often frozen or covered with snow, red-headed woodpeckers and flickers move south, while tree-foraging woodpeckers haunt the northern woods throughout the year. The sapsucker, another migratory woodpecker, feeds on cambium tissue (which it exposes from under the tree's protective outer bark), flowing sap, and active insects that are attracted to the sap. It, too, retreats to the south as temperatures drop in the north.

There are twenty-two species of nuthatches worldwide, four of which live in North America. These stocky birds typically mate for life and live throughout the year within a feeding territory of twenty-five to fifty acres.

The brown-headed nuthatch, a resident of the southeastern states, may be unique among North American birds, since it uses tools to obtain food. This diminutive bird sometimes holds a piece of bark in its bill, which it uses to pry off bark flakes to uncover hiding insects. Nuthatches also eat seeds at feeders—especially sunflower seeds— that have a high oil content akin to the fatty insect pupae and eggs which they obtain from tree bark.

Tree trunks are also frequented by the black-and-white warbler, the only tree-clinging warbler. The bold black-and-white patterns of this tiny warbler help it stay camouflaged against the contrasting tree trunk, just as most other tree-clinging woodpeckers are also patterned in black-and-white stripes. Black-and-white warblers frequent both the main trunks of the trees and large branches, sometimes acting like creepers, other times more like nuthatches. This capable bird can maneuver head-on or head-down on tree trunks, gleaning insects in just about any posture.

December 1994 / January 1995

DECEMBER

S	M	T	W	T	F	S
				1	2	3
4	5	6	7	8	9	10
11	12	13	14	15	16	17
18	19	20	21	22	23	24
25	26	27	28	29	30	31

JANUARY

S	M	T	W	T	F	S
1	2	3	4	5	6	7
8	9	10	11	12	13	14
15	16	17	18	19	20	21
22	23	24	25	26	27	28
29	30	31				

26 MONDAY   Boxing Day (Canada)

27 TUESDAY

28 WEDNESDAY

29 THURSDAY

30 FRIDAY

31 SATURDAY

1 SUNDAY   New Moon

New Year's Day

Horned puffin (*Fratercula corniculata*). Round Island, Alaska. Nikon F4 with 500mm lens, Fujichrome RDP-100 at 1/250 second/F5.6. By Jo Overholt.

January 1995

JANUARY						
S	M	T	W	T	F	S
1	2	3	4	5	6	7
8	9	10	11	12	13	14
15	16	17	18	19	20	21
22	23	24	25	26	27	28
29	30	31				

2 MONDAY

3 TUESDAY

4 WEDNESDAY

5 THURSDAY

6 FRIDAY

7 SATURDAY

8 SUNDAY

First Quarter

MONDAY 9

TUESDAY 10

WEDNESDAY 11

THURSDAY 12

FRIDAY 13

SATURDAY 14

SUNDAY 15

January 1995

JANUARY

S	M	T	W	T	F	S
1	2	3	4	5	6	7
8	9	10	11	12	13	14
15	16	17	18	19	20	21
22	23	24	25	26	27	28
29	30	31				

16 MONDAY

Full Moon

○

Martin Luther King, Jr.'s
Birthday *observed*

17 TUESDAY

18 WEDNESDAY

19 THURSDAY

20 FRIDAY

21 SATURDAY

22 SUNDAY

Red-headed woodpecker (*Melanerpes erythrocephalus*). Oak Openings Preserve, Metropark, Toledo, Ohio. Nikon F4 with 500mm lens, Fujichrome 100 at 1/60 second/F5.6. By Sharon Cummings.

Did You Know That:

* The male emperor penguin incubates its single egg for two months from the time it is laid until it hatches by balancing it on one of its webbed feet.

* The middle claw of nighthawks, some herons, barn owls, and a few others has a special "comb" on the inner edge of its central toe that may be used for scratching and removing parasites.

* A tundra swan holds the record for having the largest number of feathers—25,216. Ruby-throated hummingbirds may have the fewest—940.

* House sparrows have 11.5 percent fewer feathers in summer than in winter.

* The Atlantic puffin can hold up to sixty-two fish in its beak at one time.

* The minimum speed necessary for a bird to remain airborne is about 11 miles per hour. House sparrows are among the world's slowest flying birds at 16 to 19 miles per hour. The spine-tailed swift of India holds the record for the fastest straight-forward, wing-beating flight at 218 miles per hour.

* The alpine chough, a crowlike bird of India, lives higher than any other bird. It nests on Mount Everest at 27,000 feet.

* With the exception of shrews, birds eat more food per ounce of body weight than any other animal. Woodcocks can eat their own weight in worms each day. Black-and-white warblers may eat 80 percent of their weight in food each day.

* The stomach of a mallard duck shot in Louisiana contained 102,400 willow seeds, enough to plant two-and-a-half acres. A captive bobwhite quail ate 568 mosquitoes in two hours.

JANUARY

S	M	T	W	T	F	S
1	2	3	4	5	6	7
8	9	10	11	12	13	14
15	16	17	18	19	20	21
22	23	24	25	26	27	28
29	30	31				

January 1995

Last Quarter

◑

MONDAY *23*

TUESDAY *24*

WEDNESDAY *25*

THURSDAY *26*

FRIDAY *27*

SATURDAY *28*

SUNDAY *29*

January /
February 1995

J A N U A R Y						
S	M	T	W	T	F	S
1	2	3	4	5	6	7
8	9	10	11	12	13	14
15	16	17	18	19	20	21
22	23	24	25	26	27	28
29	30	31				

F E B R U A R Y						
S	M	T	W	T	F	S
			1	2	3	4
5	6	7	8	9	10	11
12	13	14	15	16	17	18
19	20	21	22	23	24	25
26	27	28				

30 MONDAY   New Moon
                                                 ●

31 TUESDAY

1 WEDNESDAY

2 THURSDAY

3 FRIDAY

4 SATURDAY

5 SUNDAY

White-breasted nuthatch (*Sitta carolinensis*). Great Smoky Mountains National Park, Tennessee. Pentax PZ-1 with 300mm EDIF lens, Fujichrome Velvia at 1/30 second/F5.6. By Adam Jones.

Chickenlike Marsh Birds

RAILS ARE symbolic of marshes. Their long legs and toes, flexible wings, and "thin as a rail" frames permit them to slip through dense vegetation. A unique clawlike appendage at the tip of the bend in the wing also helps the rail maneuver through tangles of grass and sedge. Although they are pathetic flyers, rails can quickly outmaneuver clumsy humans in their habitat. When pursued, they seldom fly, but simply lower their heads, stretch forward, and thread their way through the thickest grasses with incredible speed.

Rails are fearless creatures when it comes to repelling rivals from their territory. Rails of nearly all species have at one time or another stepped out of the camouflage of marsh grass onto the boot of a birder who was broadcasting a tape recording of rail calls. Yet these are rare events; more often the rails lurk silently among the emergents, out of view, likely enjoying their elusiveness. Rails are usually brown or gray in color, with streaked plumage that gives them added camouflage.

One of the best rail-finding techniques is to scan carefully the edges of ditches that cut through the marsh. Salt marsh rails like the clapper rail are easiest to see, since tidal pools trap crabs and minnows that tempt the rails out of their usual dense cover. With ample patience you will eventually see the clappers venture out to explore the low-tide mud. If a canoe is available, use it to slip back into the marsh and wait for the rails to emerge. This is the best way to see them.

If patience fails, open your field guide and slap it shut! The resulting crack may disturb a clapper enough to make it call. The actual clapper voice may incite neighbors to respond. In fresh-water habitats, try taking two rocks and banging them together to make a clicking sound. This mimics the "kidik-kidik" call of the Virginia rail. Dawn and dusk are the best times for rail watching, as the birds are more active and more vocal at these hours.

King rails, considered by some to be a fresh-water form of the clapper rail, are the largest of the North American rails. King rails frequent fresh-water marshes in most of eastern North America, but are most abundant in tidal marshes along the Atlantic and Gulf coastal plains. Black rails are the smallest North American rail, just five inches long—about the size of a sparrow. They are seldom seen, perhaps because they resemble a mouse dashing through the salt marsh. Listen for them at night in spartina meadows: "Kick-ee-doo" and "did-ee-duck" are their favorite messages.

There are 132 species of rails, gallinules, and coots world-wide. Of these, 13 species occur in North America. All rails can swim and dive, but coots (the most aquatic rails) are as capable on open water as ducks. Their lobed toes resemble the toes of grebes rather than those of other rails. Coots can dive to twenty-five feet and stay underwater for up to sixteen seconds.

Gallinules are midway in structure between the long-legged, narrow-bodied rails and the aquatic coots and are capable on both open water and dense vegetation.

Because rails, coots, and gallinules are migratory, but weak flyers, they sometimes end up on oceanic islands where they develop into distinct species. In the absence of predators, they may even lose their ability to fly. Isolation on islands has led to many species with limited ranges, like the Hawaiian coot, the Aldabra rail, and the Marianas gallinule. When these isolated birds meet people and their associated dogs, cats, and rats, their future becomes imperiled. Sixteen species of rails, coots, and gallinules are presently threatened with extinction.

February 1995

FEBRUARY						
S	M	T	W	T	F	S
			1	2	3	4
5	6	7	8	9	10	11
12	13	14	15	16	17	18
19	20	21	22	23	24	25
26	27	28				

6 MONDAY

7 TUESDAY   First Quarter

8 WEDNESDAY

9 THURSDAY

10 FRIDAY

11 SATURDAY

12 SUNDAY

February 1995

MONDAY *13*

Valentine's Day

TUESDAY *14*

Full Moon
○

WEDNESDAY *15*

THURSDAY *16*

FRIDAY *17*

SATURDAY *18*

SUNDAY *19*

February 1995

F E B R U A R Y						
S	M	T	W	T	F	S
			1	2	3	4
5	6	7	8	9	10	11
12	13	14	15	16	17	18
19	20	21	22	23	24	25
26	27	28				

20 MONDAY   Presidents' Day

21 TUESDAY

22 WEDNESDAY   Last Quarter

23 THURSDAY

24 FRIDAY

25 SATURDAY

26 SUNDAY

King rail (*Rallus elegans*) emerging from black grass (*Juncus gerardi*). Great Island Marsh, Old Lyme, Connecticut. Olympus FTL with 200mm lens, Kodachrome 25 at 1/15 second/F16. By William Burt.

Did You Know That:

- Acorn woodpeckers chisel tight-fitting holes for individual acorns in favorite caching trees. One huge ponderosa pine in the San Jacinto Mountains of California contained 50,000 acorns, each tucked into a customized cavity.

- The first fossil bird found in North America was a snipelike bird discovered in marl (crumbling clay and calcium) beds near Arneyville, New Jersey, in 1834. The fossil bird was about 130 million years old.

- Fossil remains prove that an extinct, 40-to-50-pound giant vulture with a wingspan of 12 feet once soared through the skies of California, Florida, and Mexico. The largest bird ever to fly was likely a vulture known from a fossil record in Nevada—*Teratornis incredibilis,* which had a 16.5-foot wingspan. By contrast, the endangered California condor has a wingspan of 10 feet.

- Heartbeat increases as the weight of the bird decreases. Wild turkeys weigh in at about 8,750 grams and have a heartbeat of 93 beats per minute. Ruby-throated hummingbirds weigh just 4 grams and have a heartbeat of 615 beats per minute.

- To cool themselves, most birds start panting when air temperature reaches about 105 degrees F. Vultures and storks also find relief from heat by defecating on their legs.

- In an experiment on homing, a Laysan albatross was taken from its nest on Midway Island, northwest of Hawaii, and flown to the Philippines, 4,120 miles away. Even though these albatross do not normally visit the Philippines, the bird made its way back to Midway Island 32 days later.

- About 50 percent of the flicker's diet consists of ants. Five thousand ants were once found in the stomach of a single flicker.

FEBRUARY						
S	M	T	W	T	F	S
			1	2	3	4
5	6	7	8	9	10	11
12	13	14	15	16	17	18
19	20	21	22	23	24	25
26	27	28				

MARCH						
S	M	T	W	T	F	S
			1	2	3	4
5	6	7	8	9	10	11
12	13	14	15	16	17	18
19	20	21	22	23	24	25
26	27	28	29	30	31	

February / March 1995

MONDAY 27

TUESDAY 28

New Moon

●

Ash Wednesday

WEDNESDAY 1

THURSDAY 2

FRIDAY 3

SATURDAY 4

SUNDAY 5

Ducklike Birds

MOST LOONS, grebes, and ducks start migrating toward nesting areas in March. After wintering on open water from the Finger Lakes of New York south to the coastal waters of the Atlantic, Gulf Coast and Pacific wetlands, and Mexico, they start their epic journey north to the promised land of prairie potholes and tundra pools. This northward movement is set in rhythm by lengthening days that trigger the interaction of two hormones—prolactin of the pituitary gland, and corticosterone. While lengthening days urge waterbirds to begin their migration, the pace of migration is fine-tuned as birds search for open water on their way north. During the spring migration, waterfowl often overfly the northern limit of open water and discover frozen ponds, necessitating a temporary retreat to the south.

Loons belong to an ancient group which dates back about 130 million years. Ancient loons probably coexisted with dinosaurs. There are four living loon species worldwide, and all occur in North America. Loons look something like grebes, another ducklike bird, but they are not closely related.

The differences between the two groups are conspicuous at every stage of the life cycle. For example, grebe eggs are unspotted and hence vulnerable to predators, but parents cover the eggs when they leave the nest unattended. In contrast, loons lay spotted eggs and leave them uncovered when they leave their nests. Soon after hatching, young grebes and loons ride their parents' backs, in part because their down is not waterproof. Loon chicks are a uniform, sooty gray, while grebes have a striped appearance.

While both loons and grebes are master divers, their foot shapes reflect important differences. Loons have fully webbed toes, while grebes have scaled lobes extending from their toes. Both groups are capable divers, but each has its favorite haunts. Loons frequent deep waters, diving to depths of 240 feet, while the smaller grebes generally dive into shallower water, with each grebe species feeding at different depths, depending largely on its weight.

Loons and grebes look something like ducks, but ducks, geese, and swans comprise their own, distinct order, called waterfowl. Distinguished from loons and grebes by their rounded beaks, waterfowl far outnumber the other ducklike birds. North America is home to about

90 million ducks of thirty-six species, about 3 to 4 million geese of seven species, and about 150,000 swans of two species.

Most waterfowl migrate throughout the night into the early morning hours at speeds of 40 to 60 miles per hour, although geese may migrate during both day and night. Band recoveries show that during their fall migration, waterfowl may move at the rate of 1,000 miles per month, but some blue-winged teal can move at much faster speeds of 2,000 to 3,000 miles per month.

Female ducks usually return to the vicinity of their hatching place two to three years after hatching. They pair with males in their winter home and the male heads north with the hen. Since pairs seldom mate together more than once, the male may visit many regions of North America over its adult life. Females build nests and incubate the eggs without assistance from the males. Some hens, like eiders, usually stay with their eggs for a month while they are incubating.

The future of waterfowl in North America is intimately linked to the well-being of wetlands, those shallow-water habitats that include estuaries, fresh and salt marshes, and ponds. Acre by acre, wetlands are being converted to farmland, housing developments, and parking lots at the rate of about 500,000 acres each year. North American wetlands have been reduced from about 127 million acres to about 92 million acres in the lower forty-eight states.

Although wetlands cover only about 5 percent of the country's land area, a third of all North American birds depend on wetland habitats. As wetlands shrink, the remaining habitat may trap surviving waterfowl, crowding them together where they will be increasingly vulnerable to diseases such as tuberculosis and predation from foxes and raccoons.

March 1995

MARCH

S	M	T	W	T	F	S
			1	2	3	4
5	6	7	8	9	10	11
12	13	14	15	16	17	18
19	20	21	22	23	24	25
26	27	28	29	30	31	

6 MONDAY

7 TUESDAY

8 WEDNESDAY

9 THURSDAY   First Quarter

10 FRIDAY

11 SATURDAY

12 SUNDAY

Common loon (*Gavia immer*) and young. Northern Light Lake near Thunder Bay, Ontario, Canada. Nikon F4 with 600mm lens, Kodachrome 64 at 1/125 second/F8. By Wayne and Helen Lankinen.

March 1995

MARCH						
S	M	T	W	T	F	S
			1	2	3	4
5	6	7	8	9	10	11
12	13	14	15	16	17	18
19	20	21	22	23	24	25
26	27	28	29	30	31	

13 MONDAY

14 TUESDAY

15 WEDNESDAY

16 THURSDAY   Full Moon
                                                    ○

17 FRIDAY   St. Patrick's Day

18 SATURDAY

19 SUNDAY

Equinox

MONDAY 20

TUESDAY 21

WEDNESDAY 22

Last Quarter

THURSDAY 23

FRIDAY 24

SATURDAY 25

SUNDAY 26

March /
April 1995

		MARCH				
S	M	T	W	T	F	S
			1	2	3	4
5	6	7	8	9	10	11
12	13	14	15	16	17	18
19	20	21	22	23	24	25
26	27	28	29	30	31	

		APRIL				
S	M	T	W	T	F	S
						1
2	3	4	5	6	7	8
9	10	11	12	13	14	15
16	17	18	19	20	21	22
23/30	24	25	26	27	28	29

27 MONDAY

28 TUESDAY

29 WEDNESDAY

30 THURSDAY   New Moon
                                                ●

31 FRIDAY

1 SATURDAY

2 SUNDAY   Daylight Saving
                                     Time Begins

Female hooded merganser (*Lophodytes cucullatus*). Pearl River basin near Jackson, Mississippi. Nikon FM2 with 500mm lens, Kodachrome 64 at 1/125 second/F4. By Joe Mac Hudspeth, Jr.

Hovering Birds

HUMMINGBIRDS ARE best known for their hovering skills, but other birds, such as kingfishers, kestrels, rough-legged hawks, and ospreys also hover. These birds hover in place to watch for prey, then plunge to the ground or into the water to grab their meal.

Large birds hover by holding their bodies in near vertical posture and beating their wings up and down with tail feathers depressed and spread. When ready to plunge, kestrels and kingfishers fold their wings tight and drop head-first toward their prey. Kingfishers grab fish in their beaks, while kestrels and other hawks snag their prey with outstretched talons.

Gulls are also capable of hovering. The herring gull hovers with a clam or sea urchin in its beak, then drops it on a rocky shore or parking lot, descending later to eat the contents. Ring-billed gulls sometimes hover at crabapples to pluck fruit.

While many birds hover occasionally, hummingbirds are hover-masters. Hovering permits access to deep flowers that are inaccessible to heavier birds that are unable to balance on swaying flowers. In this way hovering hummingbirds can harvest the rich supply of nectar, insects, and spiders found in colorful flowers.

Hummingbirds hover by rotating their shoulder joints and turning the pointed wings completely over on the backstroke and forward stroke. In one motion, this action slices into the air, checking movement in both forward and backward directions. In each stroke, hummers use some of the energy transferred to the air from the previous sweep of wings. The direction of thrust changes from forward to backward, working to cancel movement. Since hummer wings may buzz as fast as eighty beats per second, the bird's body is held nearly stationary.

Hummingbirds are the only birds that move their wings just at the shoulder—all others move parts of the wing at the joints of shoulder, elbow, and wrist. In contrast to other birds, hummingbirds use their entire wings as propellers. Because they rotate their wings at the shoulder, they have remarkably free movement, which gives them astonishing maneuverability. Hummingbirds can fly forward, backward, sideways, and directly up and down.

Hummingbirds show remarkable speed, diving in courtship flights of forty-seven to forty-nine miles per hour. Such flights are possible in large part because of the hummingbird's massive flight muscles, which comprise 22 to 34 percent of their body weight.

There are at least 319 species of hummingbirds on earth, all in the western hemisphere. Of these, 19 species occur in North America, but 11 range only near the Mexican border. Most North American hummingbirds spend their winter months in Central America.

Each April, ruby-throated hummingbirds migrate about 600 miles across the Gulf of Mexico. These flights are remarkable for such a small bird, but they are especially impressive because hummingbirds "burn" their food faster than any other bird and usually feed constantly during daylight. At night, their metabolism slows, and they slip into a torporlike slumber.

Just as waterfowl cannot migrate faster than they find open water, hummingbirds must not fly north faster than the opening of nectar-producing flowers. In this way, hummingbirds that frequent western mountains migrate up the mountains following the blooming of nectar-laden flowers.

On familiar territories, males perform elaborate courtship flights consisting of pendulum-like loops, wheels, and dives. Males mate with the females attracted to their performance and use similar flying displays to defend feeding areas from which they chase other hummers and even bumblebees.

Females build the tiny nest on a tree branch and usually lay two white eggs. Unassisted by the male, females establish a nesting territory from which they chase intruding males and other females.

April 1995

		APRIL				
S	M	T	W	T	F	S
						1
2	3	4	5	6	7	8
9	10	11	12	13	14	15
16	17	18	19	20	21	22
23/30	24	25	26	27	28	29

3 MONDAY

4 TUESDAY

5 WEDNESDAY

6 THURSDAY

7 FRIDAY

8 SATURDAY

First Quarter

9 SUNDAY

Palm Sunday

Male rufous hummingbird (*Selasphorus rufus*). Near Hope, British Columbia, Canada. Nikon F3 with 200mm macro lens, Kodachrome 64 at 1/60 second/F22. By Robert Lankinen.

April 1995

		APRIL				
S	M	T	W	T	F	S
						1
2	3	4	5	6	7	8
9	10	11	12	13	14	15
16	17	18	19	20	21	22
23/30	24	25	26	27	28	29

10 MONDAY

11 TUESDAY

12 WEDNESDAY

13 THURSDAY

14 FRIDAY   Good Friday

15 SATURDAY   Full Moon
                                                  ◯
                                              Passover

16 SUNDAY   Easter

Easter Monday (Canada)   MONDAY **17**

TUESDAY **18**

WEDNESDAY **19**

THURSDAY **20**

Last Quarter ◐   FRIDAY **21**

Earth Day   SATURDAY **22**

SUNDAY **23**

April 1995

APRIL						
S	M	T	W	T	F	S
						1
2	3	4	5	6	7	8
9	10	11	12	13	14	15
16	17	18	19	20	21	22
23/30	24	25	26	27	28	29

24 MONDAY

25 TUESDAY

26 WEDNESDAY

John James Audubon's
Birthday

27 THURSDAY

28 FRIDAY

Arbor Day

29 SATURDAY

New Moon
●

Annular Eclipse of the Sun
1:40 P.M. E.D.T.

30 SUNDAY

Broad-tailed hummingbird nestlings (*Selasphorus platycercus*). Walker Ranch, Boulder County Open Space, Colorado. Nikon 8008S with 105mm lens, Kodachrome 64 at 1/60 second/F22. By Charles W. Melton.

Shorebirds

SHOREBIRDS EMBODY the spring migration. By mid-May, their numbers peak on the New Jersey coast. Here, vast flocks of "peeps," composed mainly of semipalmated and least sandpipers, scamper over the mud, picking at the surface for crustaceans and worms. Dowitchers probe the deeper mud, plunging their long beaks into the mud as they search for marine worms. Greater and lesser yellowlegs wade gracefully through the shallow water, taking long, elegant strides.

Shorebirds seem so at home in this setting that it is hard to believe that this is a transitional scene. Weeks earlier, the same birds were feeding along the coasts of Argentina and Peru, and soon they will depart for tundra wetlands. Their stopover on the Jersey shore is a vital refueling stop midway between South America and the far north.

While there are many birds which frequent shores—herons, ducks, gulls, and terns—the term *shorebird* has a special meaning to birders. Depending on the taxonomist, there are between 180 and 200 species in the shorebird suborder Charadrii, representing eleven families. One third of these species, divided into six families and twenty-four genera, occur in North America. Two families, the sandpipers and plovers, contain nearly all of the North American sandpipers. Only thick-knees (wide-eyed, long-legged upland birds of central America), oystercatchers, stilts, and jacana fall outside the sandpiper and plover families.

Plovers are distinguished by their round, dovelike heads and short bodies, bills, and necks. The plover's eye is large and gentle and most species lack a functional hind toe. In contrast, sandpipers have long beaks, longer legs, and smaller eyes, and their bodies are long and pointed. Most plovers, such as killdeer and black-bellied plover, are boldly marked with uniform backs and distinct black patterns on their underparts. In contrast, sandpipers are usually speckled or striped, and their underparts are light colored.

Like falcons, both sandpipers and plovers have long, pointed wings that give them speed and streamlined form during their long migrations. The semipalmated sandpiper, one of the smallest species, can fly up to fifty miles per hour.

Most plovers and sandpipers experience a dramatic change during late winter, when they acquire their breeding plumage. While the bright patterns of knots and turnstones contrast with sandy beaches, these patterns are very cryptic and no doubt provide excellent camouflage from arctic fox, weasels, and other predators, which would have greater difficulty locating nests among lichens, crowberries, cranberries, and other low-growing plants of the high arctic.

The lesser yellowlegs lays four eggs in a well-camouflaged nest in muskeg country of scattered trees, often on dry ridges near the edge of tundra. The nests are extremely hard to find, in part because one member of the pair will sit very tight to the nest. Both male and female incubate, and the young start feeding themselves on a diet of tiny insects and worms soon after they hatch.

If the eggs or young are threatened by a predator, the parents usually perform distraction displays in which they attempt to lure the predator from the nest. The adults usually start their southbound migration before the young, leaving the young to find their way to wintering grounds on their own.

Shorebird numbers today are far fewer than those encountered by John James Audubon in 1821, when he witnessed as many as 48,000 golden plover shot for food and sport in a single day. While shorebirds are now protected by law, they remain especially vulnerable to disturbance and pollution as they migrate through populated areas, dependent on the same crowded beaches that attract humans.

May 1995

			MAY			
S	M	T	W	T	F	S
	1	2	3	4	5	6
7	8	9	10	11	12	13
14	15	16	17	18	19	20
21	22	23	24	25	26	27
28	29	30	31			

1 MONDAY

2 TUESDAY

3 WEDNESDAY

4 THURSDAY

5 FRIDAY

6 SATURDAY

7 SUNDAY   First Quarter

Lesser yellowlegs (*Tringa flavipes*). Edwin B. Forsythe National Wildlife Refuge, New Jersey. Nikon F3T with 600mm lens, Fujichrome 100 at 1/500 second/F5.6. By Gil Lopez-Espina/*Mind Alternative Productions.*

May 1995

			MAY			
S	M	T	W	T	F	S
	1	2	3	4	5	6
7	8	9	10	11	12	13
14	15	16	17	18	19	20
21	22	23	24	25	26	27
28	29	30	31			

8 MONDAY

9 TUESDAY

10 WEDNESDAY

11 THURSDAY

12 FRIDAY

13 SATURDAY

14 SUNDAY

Full Moon

○

Mother's Day

MONDAY *15*

TUESDAY *16*

WEDNESDAY *17*

THURSDAY *18*

FRIDAY *19*

SATURDAY *20*

Last Quarter

SUNDAY *21*

May 1995

MAY

S	M	T	W	T	F	S
	1	2	3	4	5	6
7	8	9	10	11	12	13
14	15	16	17	18	19	20
21	22	23	24	25	26	27
28	29	30	31			

22 MONDAY   Victoria Day (Canada)

23 TUESDAY

24 WEDNESDAY

25 THURSDAY

26 FRIDAY

27 SATURDAY

28 SUNDAY

Killdeer (*Charadrius vociferus*) with bird's-foot trefoil (*Lotus corniculatus*). Near Brainerd, Minnesota. Nikon F4 with 400mm lens, Fujichrome Velvia at 1/250 second/F5.6. By Bill Marchel.

Did You Know That:

- Belted kingfishers use their beaks and feet to excavate their nesting burrows in stream banks. In this manner, they dig a tunnel three to seven feet deep over a three-week-long period.

- Of the 215 bird species that nest in Michigan, only 20 are year-round residents.

- More than 100 species of birds that nest in the United States spend their winters in the West Indies or in Central and South America.

- Bobolinks and barn swallows have the longest migration routes of all land birds, from nesting areas in Alaska to winter homes in Argentina.

- Swallows and swifts, which can feed while flying, migrate during daylight. In contrast, most land birds that feed from the ground or pick insects off trees migrate at night, when it is cooler and they are less vulnerable to hawks.

- Sparrows that live in course grass molt all of their feathers twice each year. Ptarmigan, high-latitude grouse, molt all their feathers three times each year to obtain a brown summer plumage, an intermediate brown-and-white plumage in fall, and a pure white plumage in winter.

- Most large white birds, such as whooping cranes, gannets, white ibis, snow geese, and white pelicans, have black wing tips. Black pigment (melanin) reduces wear on the wing tips.

- A golden eagle may take two months to build its large nest of sticks, while a red-eyed vireo takes just five days to build its nest.

- Barn swallows may make more than 1,200 trips to carry mud for their nests, one mouthful at a time.

M A Y						
S	M	T	W	T	F	S
	1	2	3	4	5	6
7	8	9	10	11	12	13
14	15	16	17	18	19	20
21	22	23	24	25	26	27
28	29	30	31			

J U N E						
S	M	T	W	T	F	S
				1	2	3
4	5	6	7	8	9	10
11	12	13	14	15	16	17
18	19	20	21	22	23	24
25	26	27	28	29	30	

May / June 1995

New Moon

●

Memorial Day *observed*

MONDAY 29

TUESDAY 30

WEDNESDAY 31

THURSDAY 1

FRIDAY 2

SATURDAY 3

SUNDAY 4

Swallows and Swifts

IN MID-JUNE, swallows are busy rearing their young. Adept fliers, they have such keen eyes that they can snag tiny insects in midair. Swallows locate prey by sight, swoop in for the attack, and then open their beaks. Rictal bristles at the corners of the beak sense vibrations from flying prey, and these alert the swallow to open its beak in time to swoop up the unsuspecting insect.

There are seventy-nine species of swallows worldwide, and eleven of these nest in North America. Tree swallows are one of the most common eastern species. They are usually the first swallow to return to the northeast because they winter relatively nearby, in the southeastern states. The sexes look similar, with steely blue-green backs and immaculate white undersides. If they arrive on the nesting grounds before flying insects are available, they may eat bayberries and other fruits.

Tree swallows build a cozy nest in their selected cavity and soon line it with white breast feathers, which they scavenge from chicken yards or gull colonies. A recent study demonstrated the importance of the feather liners, showing that more young were reared in nests with feathers than in nests without feathers. Banding studies have shown that females do all of the incubation, while the male usually stays nearby, but some males deviate from this pattern and have two mates at the same time.

The closely related violet-green swallow is more colonial than the tree swallow. As many as twenty pairs have nested in abandoned woodpecker holes in the same pine tree. Like the tree swallow, violet-green pairs seldom re-form, and they often switch their nest site between years. One sixteen-year study found a different pair of swallows in the same box during each year of the study.

Swifts resemble swallows, but they are only distantly related. Swifts and hummingbirds belong to the Apodiformes—the footless birds. Swifts do have feet, but their feet and legs are extremely diminutive. Swifts can cling to trees and the insides of chimneys (aided by their spine-tipped, proplike tails), but they can barely shuffle across the ground.

In flight, swifts have a quick, fluttering wingbeat and a chirping voice, and tend to fly higher than swallows. Swallows are more colorful than swifts, which are usually ash gray or black-and-white.

While they are nearly helpless on the ground, swifts are extremely capable in the air. These highly social birds usually feed in flocks and probably spend more of their life in the air than any other bird. Swifts are so well adapted to life in the sky that they not only feed exclusively in the air, but they also court, drink, bathe, gather nesting material, and even copulate while on the wing. Aircraft pilots sometimes report that European swifts ascend to great heights at night and spend the night on the wing! Needletails, an Asian swift, fly at speeds up to 218 miles per hour, ranking them as the fastest birds.

Swifts from temperate regions are usually great migrants. European swifts may fly at least 560 miles a day during the nesting season. Similarly, a chimney swift flew an estimated 1,350,000 miles during its nine-year life of migrating from North America to wintering grounds in Peru. Swift wings have short, massive bones compared to the wings of swallows. These move in unison during forward flight and shift to an alternate flight when the bird turns. This gives the birds a rather jerky flight pattern.

Most swifts use saliva from their enlarged salivary glands to cement their nests together and to attach them to the insides of hollow trees, caves, or chimnies. While some species, like chimney swifts, have long-distance migrations, others, such as the western white-throated swift, become torpid when it becomes too cold to capture flying insects. During migration, hundreds of swifts sometimes share traditional communal roosts inside chimneys.

June 1995

JUNE
S	M	T	W	T	F	S
				1	2	3
4	5	6	7	8	9	10
11	12	13	14	15	16	17
18	19	20	21	22	23	24
25	26	27	28	29	30	

5 MONDAY

6 TUESDAY

First Quarter

7 WEDNESDAY

8 THURSDAY

9 FRIDAY

10 SATURDAY

11 SUNDAY

Tree swallows (*Tachycineta bicolor*). Assateague Island, Chincoteague National
Wildlife Refuge, Virginia. Nikon FM2 with 400mm lens, Fujichrome 50 at
1/125 second/F8. By C. Gable Ray.

June 1995

JUNE

S	M	T	W	T	F	S
				1	2	3
4	5	6	7	8	9	10
11	12	13	14	15	16	17
18	19	20	21	22	23	24
25	26	27	28	29	30	

12 MONDAY

13 TUESDAY   Full Moon
                                                ○

14 WEDNESDAY

15 THURSDAY

16 FRIDAY

17 SATURDAY

18 SUNDAY   Father's Day

June 1995

Last Quarter

◑

MONDAY *19*

TUESDAY *20*

Solstice

WEDNESDAY *21*

THURSDAY *22*

FRIDAY *23*

SATURDAY *24*

SUNDAY *25*

Did You Know That:

- More than 30 species of birds use cast-off snakeskins to line their nests.

- A brown thrasher in Minnesota lined its nest with a five-dollar bill, and a Texas white-necked raven built its nest entirely from scrap barbed wire.

- In one study, 25 percent of cliff swallow nests contained eggs from swallows other than the parents who built the nest. Some cliff swallows carry their "extra" eggs in their beaks to foster homes.

- Brown-headed cowbirds and certain African cuckoos always lay their eggs in other birds' nests. These "brood parasites" have evolved eggs that resemble the eggs of their hosts.

- Some birds clean themselves by taking dust baths. House sparrows, for example, often flutter in dusty places, using the same movements that they would use in water. Dust absorbs excess feather lipids and preening oils.

- More than 200 kinds of birds are known either to sit on live anthills or actively place live ants in their feathers. The ants apparently give off formic acid, which helps to control feather lice and other parasites.

- At least 170 kinds of birds sunbathe. Sunbathers sit on a sidewalk or other flat, sunny area, extend a wing, and lean toward the sun to "soak up rays."

- North American blackbirds, such as red-winged blackbirds and common grackles, typically sleep in roosts. Some winter roosts contain upwards of 15 million blackbirds.

- Atlantic puffins may dive to 200 feet to obtain prey. The deep-diving record belongs, however, to emperor penguins. These heavy-bodied birds can dive to 875 feet, staying down for 18 minutes.

		J U N E				
S	M	T	W	T	F	S
				1	2	3
4	5	6	7	8	9	10
11	12	13	14	15	16	17
18	19	20	21	22	23	24
25	26	27	28	29	30	

		J U L Y				
S	M	T	W	T	F	S
						1
2	3	4	5	6	7	8
9	10	11	12	13	14	15
16	17	18	19	20	21	22
23/30	24/31	25	26	27	28	29

June /
July 1995

MONDAY 26

New Moon

●

TUESDAY 27

WEDNESDAY 28

THURSDAY 29

FRIDAY 30

Canada Day

SATURDAY 1

SUNDAY 2

Hawklike Birds

HAWKLIKE BIRDS include diurnal birds of prey such as hawks, eagles, falcons, kites, and vultures. They range in size from condors to kestrels and inhabit every corner and habitat of North America. They include twenty-five species in the hawk family (four eagles, four kites, and seventeen species called hawks) as well as seven falcons, three vultures, and one osprey.

This diverse group shares one truly remarkable feature—their sense of sight. The term *hawkeye* is very appropriate, for hawks have an unparalleled ability to discern prey at great distances. Hawks have binocular vision, where the eyes are positioned somewhat toward the front of the head to permit overlapping images. Binocular vision is necessary for depth perception, and birds of prey such as hawks and owls require a keen sense of depth if they are to locate their prey successfully. This tendency is most conspicuous in owls, whose eyes are brought as far forward on their heads as are humans.

Large hawks have enormous eyes, equal in size to the eyes of adult humans. Microscopically, the avian retina has remarkable acuity. Humans have about 200,000 visual cells in a single fovea on each retina. By contrast, birds of prey have two fovea in each eye and some, like the common buteo (a European bird similar to our red-tailed hawk), have a million visual cells per square millimeter! With these statistics in mind, it is little wonder that a rough-legged hawk can hover a hundred feet over a farm field, spot the blur of a brown mouse, and plummet to earth to capture its prey.

Prairie falcons belong to the falcon family, a distinct group of hawklike birds which includes fifty-eight species worldwide. Of these, seven species occur in North America. Falcons resemble hawks, but share several distinct features. A close view shows that they have a notched beak with a round nostril and conspicuous tubercle (or nodule) in the center of the nostril. This presumably deflects air from entering the nostril as the falcons stoop at speeds over a hundred miles per hour. Falcons have long, pointed wings and long tails which enhance their streamlined shape. Their long toes fold into a stout fist which they use to stun their prey in flight before snatching it in midair.

Prairie falcons are similar in size and speed to peregrine falcons.

Unlike the peregrine, they are not migratory, but are residents of prairie country, deserts, and mountains in the western states.

Harris hawks were named for Edward Harris, a friend of John James Audubon. These spectacular birds nest in Mexico and Central and South America, as well as in the southwestern United States.

Hawks are important indicators of the presence of toxic substances in our environment. Because they feed entirely on other animals, they tend to concentrate toxins in their bodies and eggs. Following World War II, widespread use of the insecticide DDT eliminated all peregrine falcons east of the Mississippi and caused peregrine numbers to plummet in the American West. Laws now restrict the use of DDT, but it still occurs as a contaminant in Kelthane, a legal insecticide, and DDT itself is used in some Latin American countries, where it impacts both resident birds and North American migrants.

Peregrine, bald eagle, and osprey populations have rebounded as a result of a cleaner environment and the release of captive-reared young, but the lesson learned from DDT must also apply to other destructive chemicals both in the United States and abroad.

Successful public education about the aesthetic and practical benefits of birds of prey is necessary to insure that these spectacular birds will remain a conspicuous part of our surroundings.

July 1995

JULY						
S	M	T	W	T	F	S
						1
2	3	4	5	6	7	8
9	10	11	12	13	14	15
16	17	18	19	20	21	22
23/30	24/31	25	26	27	28	29

3 MONDAY

4 TUESDAY   Independence Day

5 WEDNESDAY   First Quarter

6 THURSDAY

7 FRIDAY

8 SATURDAY

9 SUNDAY

Prairie falcon (*Falco mexicanus*). Columbia plateau, Washington. Nikon F4 with 800mm lens, Fujichrome 50 at 1/125 second/F5.6. By Art Wolfe.

July 1995

		J U L Y				
S	M	T	W	T	F	S
						1
2	3	4	5	6	7	8
9	10	11	12	13	14	15
16	17	18	19	20	21	22
23/30	24/31	25	26	27	28	29

10 MONDAY

11 TUESDAY

12 WEDNESDAY   Full Moon

13 THURSDAY

14 FRIDAY

15 SATURDAY

16 SUNDAY

MONDAY *17*

TUESDAY *18*

Last Quarter

◐

WEDNESDAY *19*

THURSDAY *20*

FRIDAY *21*

SATURDAY *22*

SUNDAY *23*

July 1995

JULY

S	M	T	W	T	F	S
						1
2	3	4	5	6	7	8
9	10	11	12	13	14	15
16	17	18	19	20	21	22
23/30	24/31	25	26	27	28	29

24 MONDAY

25 TUESDAY

26 WEDNESDAY

27 THURSDAY   New Moon
                                                  ●

28 FRIDAY

29 SATURDAY

30 SUNDAY

Harris hawk (*Parabuteo unicinctus*) perching in honey mesquite tree (*Prosopis glandulosa*). West of Amistad Reservoir, Texas. Olympus OM3 with 400mm lens and 1.4× converter, Fujichrome 100 at 1/500 second/F5.6. By Rick Poley.

Gulls and Terns

AT GULL AND TERN nesting colonies, August is the culminating month of a cycle that began the previous April or May. If it has been a successful season, the colony will throb with the movements, sounds, and smells associated with the rearing of young.

Adult seabirds gather marine nutrients into their colonies, transforming some into their own bodies and some into the flesh and feathers of their young. Nutrients arrive in a constant stream from all directions in the concentrated form of small fish and invertebrates.

By August, the transformation process is nearly complete—a new seabird generation, conceived and reared from the abundance of the sea. Even the plant life benefits, sprayed and splattered by a rich supply of nitrogen fertilizer.

There are forty-three species of gulls in the world and thirty-nine kinds of terns. Of these, twenty-five species of gulls and eighteen species of terns nest in North America. Jaegers and skuas (five species) and skimmer (one species) are in separate but closely allied subfamilies.

Gulls are medium-sized seabirds with generalized beak, feet, and body shape. Along coasts, they function as oceangoing crows that scavenge garbage and fish offal as well as rob other seabird nests of eggs and chicks. Most gulls are either residents or short-distance migrants. As a group, they shun long-distance travels, preferring to stay in the vicinity of their natal home. Most gulls prefer to nest and feed in groups, hence their complex of calls, each of which has a special meaning. Skuas and jaegers are streamlined gulls and tend to be more active as predators than as scavengers.

While most gulls are in the stay-at-home crowd, terns are vagabonds. Like falcons and shorebirds, which are streamlined for long-distance travel, terns grace the air with swept-back body form, their wanderlust sharply contrasting with the resident nature of gulls.

Gulls and terns are long-lived birds. Some live to the mature age of thirty years or more, and it is not uncommon for colony members to live fifteen to twenty years.

Black terns are unusual among the terns for their dark plumage and habit of nesting in fresh water marshes. Their colonies are widespread in North America, but they are uncommon throughout their range and listed as threatened in many states. Their principal food is insects, which they catch in midair and pick off marshy vegetation. Occasionally they show up in coastal colonies of common and arctic terns, where they pirate meals by stealing fish from nestlings.

Black terns nest in small, loose colonies, sometimes laying their eggs in matted vegetation such as the roofs of muskrat houses. Loss of wetland habitat and the associated impact of mammal predators such as foxes, mink, and raccoons are the likely reasons for declining numbers of these delightful birds.

There are two species of kittiwake, the black-legged and the red-legged. Black-legged kittiwakes are abundant birds in both the North Atlantic and North Pacific oceans. They are unique among the gulls for nesting on the sides of cliffs, where they build substantial nests to cradle their eggs and chicks. While other gulls fly from their nests when predators approach, kittiwakes remain on their nests, seemingly unafraid. Likewise, young kittiwakes have the habit of remaining close to their nests, since wandering far on the steep cliffs could mean a fatal, premature fall to the sea.

Red-legged kittiwakes are rare seabirds that nest only on steep sea cliffs on the Komandorskie and Pribilof islands in the Bering Sea. The fate of these colonies is closely linked to ample food supplies.

July /
August 1995

		J U L Y				
S	M	T	W	T	F	S
						1
2	3	4	5	6	7	8
9	10	11	12	13	14	15
16	17	18	19	20	21	22
23/30	24/31	25	26	27	28	29

		A U G U S T				
S	M	T	W	T	F	S
		1	2	3	4	5
6	7	8	9	10	11	12
13	14	15	16	17	18	19
20	21	22	23	24	25	26
27	28	29	30	31		

31 MONDAY

1 TUESDAY

2 WEDNESDAY

3 THURSDAY

First Quarter

4 FRIDAY

5 SATURDAY

6 SUNDAY

Black tern (*Chlidonias niger*). Lakeview Wildlife Management Area near Ellisburg, New York. Nikon FE2 with 400mm EDIF lens, Fujichrome Velvia at 1/250 second/F4. By Marie Read.

August 1995

		A U G U S T				
S	M	T	W	T	F	S
		1	2	3	4	5
6	7	8	9	10	11	12
13	14	15	16	17	18	19
20	21	22	23	24	25	26
27	28	29	30	31		

7 MONDAY

8 TUESDAY

9 WEDNESDAY

10 THURSDAY   Full Moon
                                            ○

11 FRIDAY

12 SATURDAY

13 SUNDAY

MONDAY **14**

TUESDAY **15**

WEDNESDAY **16**

Last Quarter

THURSDAY **17**

FRIDAY **18**

SATURDAY **19**

SUNDAY **20**

August 1995

AUGUST

S	M	T	W	T	F	S
		1	2	3	4	5
6	7	8	9	10	11	12
13	14	15	16	17	18	19
20	21	22	23	24	25	26
27	28	29	30	31		

21 MONDAY

22 TUESDAY

23 WEDNESDAY

24 THURSDAY

25 FRIDAY

26 SATURDAY

New Moon

27 SUNDAY

Red-legged kittiwake (*Rissa brevirostris*). Zapadni Rookery, St. Paul Island, Alaska.
Canon T90 with 500mm lens, Fujichrome 100 at 1/250 second/F8.
By Harold and Kathy Lindstrom.

Did You Know That:

* European starlings have unique beak muscles. While most birds have muscles that help to clamp their beaks shut, the starling has powerful muscles that help it spring its beak open! In this way it can pry open seeds and spread vegetation as it searches for prey.

* European starlings, purple martins, and red-shouldered hawks use green plants with insecticidal properties to line their nests.

* While most black-crowned night herons eat fish, others specialize in eating newly hatched tern, eider, and gull chicks.

* Parental instincts are so strong in some birds that when they lose their own young, they may adopt others. A northern cardinal once adopted a school of gaping goldfish after it lost its brood.

* The red shoulder patches of red-winged blackbirds are important for status and identity. During experiments, most red-winged blackbirds whose patches were painted black lost their territories to blackbirds with red shoulders.

* Some birds live to remarkable ages. For example, a Laysan albatross lived to 37 years, an arctic tern to 34 years, a blue jay to 16 years, and a ruby-throated hummingbird to 9 years.

* In the summer of 1956, a northern pike leaped into the air from the waters of Lake Minnetonka, Minnesota, and caught a black tern, which it dragged below the surface.

* Eating can be dangerous. Six young common terns that had just learned how to capture their own food were found dead in their nesting colony on Long Island, New York. Close inspection revealed that each had consumed a small blowfish that had inflated in its throat.

	AUGUST					
S	M	T	W	T	F	S
		1	2	3	4	5
6	7	8	9	10	11	12
13	14	15	16	17	18	19
20	21	22	23	24	25	26
27	28	29	30	31		

	SEPTEMBER					
S	M	T	W	T	F	S
					1	2
3	4	5	6	7	8	9
10	11	12	13	14	15	16
17	18	19	20	21	22	23
24	25	26	27	28	29	30

August / September 1995

MONDAY 28

TUESDAY 29

WEDNESDAY 30

THURSDAY 31

FRIDAY 1

SATURDAY 2

First Quarter
◑

SUNDAY 3

Upland Ground Birds

FOR UPLAND ground birds such as grouse, ptarmigan, prairie chickens, turkeys, and quail, fall is the season to build up fat reserves for the long winter months. Fat is especially important for the northern grouse and turkeys that occupy snowy habitats, where food is scarce during winter. In late summer and early fall they fatten on insects, wild berries, wild grapes, and nuts. These energy reserves permit the birds to fast for remarkable periods when the hardships of winter snow and ice arrive. Wild turkeys, for example, can fast for a week, and ring-necked pheasants can fast for two weeks or more.

Ptarmigan are high-latitude grouse that have several unique adaptations to snow-covered habitats. All three North American ptarmigan not only put on extra fat for the winter but molt their summer plumage of brown feathers, taking on almost completely white plumage for the winters.

The ptarmigan's winter garb also features special "snowshoes" that let them strut across their snowy landscape. In winter, most grouse acquire enlarged scales along their toes that help to spread their weight on the snowy surface. For winter walking, ptarmigan also grow dense feathers above and below the foot that provide both insulation and more surface area. These prevent the foot from sinking deeply into the snow.

Ptarmigan and grouse are members of the galliform order, along with turkeys, pheasants, and quail. They are ground-living birds that cannot swim and are comparatively weak flyers. While they will win no prizes for endurance swimming or flying, these birds are adept on foot and can outdistance most of their predators by running through dense brush. Their feet are often armed with spurs, and they have long toes that help them dig into the ground.

The Galliformes include 256 species, 30 of which live in North America. Twelve of the 30 North American species are exotics that were introduced as "game birds." These include pheasants, francolins, junglefowl, peafowl, and guineafowl.

North American grouse include both forest and grassland birds. Males in both groups perform elaborate performances to entice females during the mating season. The ruffed grouse of the eastern deciduous forests climbs onto a fallen tree during the first warm days of March and April to proclaim its territory and attract mates. The drumming starts with slow, deliberate thumping sounds which soon speed into a muffled roar. This deep, throbbing sound can be heard at any hour of the day or night.

The male grouse makes the sound by cupping its wings and striking them against the air. The drumming is of such a low frequency (forty cycles per second) that human listeners have difficulty determining their distance from the drumming bird. The low frequency may explain why great horned owls rarely kill drumming grouse, since the owl's hearing range only goes down to sixty cycles per second.

Prairie chickens, sharp-tailed grouse, and sage grouse attract mates to traditional courtship arenas called leks, where the males perform ritualized dances to attract attention and obtain matings with females. These birds of open grassland combine dramatic visual displays and performances with booming and cackling sounds to outcompete other males for the attention of females. Lek courtships are a dramatic example of sexual selection, where the females make the vital choice of which male will father their young.

Usually the dominant male claims the central position in the lek and mates with most of the females, while the males lower in the social hierarchy dance at the edge of the lek and rarely mate. In one study about a third of the males performed three-quarters of the copulations. In another study, the dominant male was a partner in seventeen of twenty-four observed matings.

September 1995

SEPTEMBER

S	M	T	W	T	F	S
					1	2
3	4	5	6	7	8	9
10	11	12	13	14	15	16
17	18	19	20	21	22	23
24	25	26	27	28	29	30

4 MONDAY   Labor Day

5 TUESDAY

6 WEDNESDAY

7 THURSDAY

8 FRIDAY   Full Moon
                                                ○

9 SATURDAY

10 SUNDAY

Gambel's quail cock (*Callipepla gambelli*) standing on staghorn cholla (*Opuntia versicolor*). Saguaro National Monument, Tucson, Arizona. Nikon F3 with 600mm lens, Kodachrome 64 at 1/125 second/F11. By G. C. Kelley.

September 1995

SEPTEMBER

S	M	T	W	T	F	S
					1	2
3	4	5	6	7	8	9
10	11	12	13	14	15	16
17	18	19	20	21	22	23
24	25	26	27	28	29	30

11 MONDAY

12 TUESDAY

13 WEDNESDAY

14 THURSDAY

15 FRIDAY

16 SATURDAY

Last Quarter

17 SUNDAY

MONDAY *18*

TUESDAY *19*

WEDNESDAY *20*

THURSDAY *21*

FRIDAY *22*

Equinox

SATURDAY *23*

New Moon

SUNDAY *24*

September / October 1995

		SEPTEMBER			
S	M	T	W	T	F	S
					1	2
3	4	5	6	7	8	9
10	11	12	13	14	15	16
17	18	19	20	21	22	23
24	25	26	27	28	29	30

		OCTOBER			
S	M	T	W	T	F	S
1	2	3	4	5	6	7
8	9	10	11	12	13	14
15	16	17	18	19	20	21
22	23	24	25	26	27	28
29	30	31				

25 MONDAY   Rosh Hashanah

26 TUESDAY

27 WEDNESDAY

28 THURSDAY

29 FRIDAY

30 SATURDAY

1 SUNDAY   First Quarter

Willow ptarmigan (*Lagopus lagopus*). Primrose Ridge, Denali National Park, Alaska.
Nikon F4 with 200–400mm lens, Kodachrome 64 at 1/125 second/F11.
By Tim Christie.

Owls

IN THIS Halloween season, we can trace some of the tales of "ghosties and ghoulies and things that go bump in the night" to owls, especially the barn owls, which sometimes inhabit the spookiest of human haunts—church steeples, abandoned houses, and hollow trees in cemeteries. Imagine entering with wide eyes the upper levels of a potentially haunted house only to hear screams and chainlike clinking sounds, and then to glimpse a white, silent form slipping away into a distant corner of the house! Would you follow?

Those fortunate enough to study barn owls in the wild are unanimous about their uncanny ability to capture food, find mates, and rear their young in total darkness. In short, owls are formidable hunters that maneuver with ease in a world where we are completely incompetent and vulnerable.

A large part of their success comes from their ability to fly silently without the usual rush of wind created by flapping wings. The secret of their silent flight lies mainly with the shape of the leading wing feather. This primary feather has serration along its outward vane—a trait that disrupts the flow of air over the wing, eliminating the vortex noise that usually results when air rushes over a smooth surface. This feature combined with soft feathers that have a high "fluff factor" gives the owls a surprise edge over their prey.

But how do owls find prey in total darkness? Barn owls have shown that they can locate and capture live mice in totally dark, soundproofed rooms. Barn owls use their disk-shaped faces to funnel sound toward their sensitive ears. When owls hear a likely sound that could reveal the location of prey, they turn toward it and accurately pinpoint its location to within 1.5 degrees in both horizontal and vertical directions.

Barn owls can determine if a sound comes from the right or left by judging the delay in time it takes for the sound to reach their asymmetrical ears. When the sound is directly ahead, it arrives at the ears simultaneously, a fact that the owl uses to orient itself toward the prey before leaving its perch. Owls also use the intensity of the sound to determine a vertical position. When a sound is equally loud in both ears, it must be at eye level.

Because barn owls are nonmigratory, they become intimately familiar with the details of their habitat—just as a blind person at home becomes familiar with his or her surroundings. Familiarity, coupled with a keen sense of sight, helps them to locate nonmoving features of their habitat, such as trees, rock formations, and rivers.

There are two families of owls in the world: barn owls and "typical owls." They are distinguished chiefly by differences in skull structure. There are 11 species of barn owls worldwide. Viewed as a group, barn owls have the widest distribution of any bird in the world, occurring on all continents and on many remote ocean islands. The typical owls include familiar owls such as the great horned and the screech owl among some 140 species. From this total, only one species of barn owl occurs across North America, along with 18 species from the typical owl family.

Great horned owls belong to the typical owl group. Unlike the barn owl, they require some light and use their huge eyes as well as their ears to locate prey. These are large birds with a wingspan of up to thirty-three inches. Although they eat mainly rats, mice, and squirrels, their bulk and power enable them to kill prey as large as skunks and house cats. These powerful birds start laying eggs in January and February. Both parents incubate the eggs for about a month and tend their two to three young for the next two months.

October 1995

OCTOBER

S	M	T	W	T	F	S
1	2	3	4	5	6	7
8	9	10	11	12	13	14
15	16	17	18	19	20	21
22	23	24	25	26	27	28
29	30	31				

2 MONDAY

3 TUESDAY

4 WEDNESDAY   Yom Kippur

5 THURSDAY

6 FRIDAY

7 SATURDAY

8 SUNDAY   Full Moon

Barn owl (*Tyto alba*). Northern Sacramento Valley, California. Canon F-1 with 300mm lens, Kodachrome 64 at 1/30 second/F11. By John Hendrickson.

October 1995

OCTOBER

S	M	T	W	T	F	S
1	2	3	4	5	6	7
8	9	10	11	12	13	14
15	16	17	18	19	20	21
22	23	24	25	26	27	28
29	30	31				

9 MONDAY

Columbus Day *observed*
Thanksgiving (Canada)

10 TUESDAY

11 WEDNESDAY

12 THURSDAY

13 FRIDAY

14 SATURDAY

15 SUNDAY

Last Quarter

◑

MONDAY **16**

TUESDAY **17**

WEDNESDAY **18**

THURSDAY **19**

FRIDAY **20**

SATURDAY **21**

SUNDAY **22**

October 1995

OCTOBER

S	M	T	W	T	F	S
1	2	3	4	5	6	7
8	9	10	11	12	13	14
15	16	17	18	19	20	21
22	23	24	25	26	27	28
29	30	31				

23 MONDAY

24 TUESDAY   New Moon
●

25 WEDNESDAY

26 THURSDAY

27 FRIDAY

28 SATURDAY

29 SUNDAY   Daylight Saving Time Ends

Great horned owl (*Bubo virginianus*). Near Howell, Michigan. Canon EOS A2E with 35–350mm lens, Fujichrome Velvia at 1/125 second/F8. By Claudia Adams.

Did You Know That:

+ Each year, tiger sharks arrive off certain Hawaiian islands just in time to eat the fledgling Laysan albatross.

+ Clark's nutcrackers, jaylike birds of the western mountains, will bury pinecones and seeds during the fall. When food supplies become scarce, they usually remember exactly where they cached their food—even after it is covered by eight inches of snow.

+ Winter forest birds such as chickadees, nuthatches, and woodpeckers often flock together when feeding. The flocks benefit by having more eyes for watching predators. Feeding efficiency also increases because individual birds spend less time looking for predators and more time searching for food.

+ Green-backed herons sometimes lure fish within striking distance by first dropping crackers and bread into the water. The bait brings the fish to the surface where these short-legged herons can better reach their next meal.

+ Fourteen species of herons stir the bottom mud to spook fish and other prey into the range of their sharp beaks.

+ Forty to sixty million years ago, seven-foot-tall giant, flightless birds called *Diatryma giganteum* stomped through what is now New Mexico. With a head as large as a horse's, a massive hooked beak, and legs more robust than an ostrich's, *Diatryma* was the largest and most powerful predatory bird ever known.

+ Bird lice often carry their own parasites—mites—which do little harm to the lice. Lice often move from one bird to the next by riding on specialized flies called hippoboscid flies that live in bird feathers.

O C T O B E R						
S	M	T	W	T	F	S
1	2	3	4	5	6	7
8	9	10	11	12	13	14
15	16	17	18	19	20	21
22	23	24	25	26	27	28
29	30	31				

N O V E M B E R						
S	M	T	W	T	F	S
			1	2	3	4
5	6	7	8	9	10	11
12	13	14	15	16	17	18
19	20	21	22	23	24	25
26	27	28	29	30		

October / November 1995

First Quarter

◖

MONDAY 30

Halloween

TUESDAY 31

WEDNESDAY 1

THURSDAY 2

FRIDAY 3

SATURDAY 4

SUNDAY 5

Long-Legged Wading Birds

DEEP IN the cypress swamps of the National Audubon Society's Corkscrew Swamp Sanctuary, a wood stork slowly wades through black waters, framed by Spanish moss and pineapple-like bromeliads. The Corkscrew, as locals call it, is home to the largest remaining colony of wood storks in Florida—a timeless setting for storks that have graced the earth for some 65 million years.

Storks, herons, and cranes have long legs for wading through shallow waters and stalking through tall grasses. They also have similar-shaped beaks, ideal for spearing fish, frogs, and insects. These similarities, however, are the result of converging lifestyles in similar habitats and mask differences revealing their dissimilar histories. Storks, herons, and ibis comprise distinct families within the same order; collectively, they include most of the wading birds in North America.

There are sixty-three species of herons worldwide, of which thirteen nest in North America. All have long legs and necks and most feed in or near water except for the insect-eating cattle egrets, which are more often found in farm fields where they eat insects flushed by grazing cattle. Herons and egrets usually curve their necks while standing. In flight, they support their heads against their backs with their necks looped. Egrets are white herons named for their elegant back feather plumes called aigrettes. Bitterns are stripe-necked herons patterned more for camouflage than show.

In contrast to the loop-necked herons, cranes, ibis, and storks extend their heads forward while in flight. Storks and ibis are closely related to herons, each making up a distinct family within the heron order, while cranes are in their own order with rails and limpkins.

Fifteen species of cranes occur worldwide, with members found on every continent except South America. The cranes include some of the most spectacular birds on earth. They are noted for their loud voices, which they freely use in flight for trumpeting that can carry with the wind for several miles. The endangered whooping crane was named for its trumpeting voice. Whoopers produce their resonant calls by passing air through five feet of convoluted windpipe that lies looped within the keel of their breastbone. Cranes migrate by day and night, often for hundreds of miles without stopping to rest.

During these olympic-like flights, cranes often fly at heights up to 13,000 feet.

Sandhill cranes are unique to North America. There are six sandhill crane subspecies, three that are nonmigratory and three that migrate. The resident birds have small, vulnerable populations in Florida, Cuba, and Mississippi. The migratory sandhill cranes are more numerous, but these birds face grave risks in transit between wintering areas on the Gulf of Mexico and their arctic homes. They are specially vulnerable during their migration bottleneck on the Platte River of Nebraska.

Each spring in mid-March, about 500,000 sandhills crowd onto the Platte River and adjacent farmland as they prepare for their final flight north to tundra nesting areas in Canada, Alaska, and Siberia. However, dams along the Platte have changed the ecology of the river, greatly reducing the amount of crane habitat, forcing the birds to forage on remnant grains in farm fields rather than prairie marshes and potholes. The National Audubon Society's Lillian Annette Rowe Sanctuary provides vital feeding and roosting places for the cranes on their marathon migration.

Long-legged wading birds are symbols of the conservation movement. In the early 1900s the plume-bird slaughter in the Everglades prompted the formation of the National Audubon Society. Although the plume birds are protected from blatant slaughter for their feathers, their numbers are at all-time lows throughout Florida and the Everglades. Today the birds are safe from hunting but vulnerable to the insatiable human thirst for the very water in which they live.

November 1995

NOVEMBER

S	M	T	W	T	F	S
			1	2	3	4
5	6	7	8	9	10	11
12	13	14	15	16	17	18
19	20	21	22	23	24	25
26	27	28	29	30		

6 MONDAY

7 TUESDAY

Full Moon

○

Election Day

8 WEDNESDAY

9 THURSDAY

10 FRIDAY

11 SATURDAY

Veterans Day
Remembrance Day (Canada)

12 SUNDAY

Limpkin (*Aramus guarauna*) with apple snail (*Pomacea paludosa*). Wakulla River, Wakulla Springs, Florida. Nikon F3 with 400mm lens, Kodachrome 64 at 250 seconds/F8. By Laura Riley.

November 1995

NOVEMBER

S	M	T	W	T	F	S
			1	2	3	4
5	6	7	8	9	10	11
12	13	14	15	16	17	18
19	20	21	22	23	24	25
26	27	28	29	30		

13 MONDAY

14 TUESDAY

15 WEDNESDAY

Last Quarter ◗

16 THURSDAY

17 FRIDAY

18 SATURDAY

19 SUNDAY

MONDAY 20

TUESDAY 21

New Moon
●

WEDNESDAY 22

Thanksgiving

THURSDAY 23

FRIDAY 24

SATURDAY 25

SUNDAY 26

November /
December 1995

NOVEMBER

S	M	T	W	T	F	S
			1	2	3	4
5	6	7	8	9	10	11
12	13	14	15	16	17	18
19	20	21	22	23	24	25
26	27	28	29	30		

DECEMBER

S	M	T	W	T	F	S
					1	2
3	4	5	6	7	8	9
10	11	12	13	14	15	16
17	18	19	20	21	22	23
24/31	25	26	27	28	29	30

27 MONDAY

28 TUESDAY

29 WEDNESDAY — First Quarter

30 THURSDAY

1 FRIDAY

2 SATURDAY

3 SUNDAY

Florida sandhill crane (*Grus canadensis pratensis*). Shore of Upper Lake, Myakka River State Park, Sarasota, Florida. Canon T90 with 500mm lens, Fujichrome Velvia at 1/250 second/F4.5. By Lynn M. and Lynda Stone.

Perching Birds

OPEN ANY bird field guide about half way and it will fall open to the pages separating woodpeckers and flycatchers. Most guides present the birds in an order from most "primitive" to "advanced," descriptions that roughly parallel the amount of time the various birds date back in the fossil record. Flycatchers mark the beginning of the "perching birds."

For this reason, loons lead off in most field guides, since they have the longest fossil record (dating back about 130 million years). In contrast, perching birds (also known as passerines) are the most recent order, dating back to the beginning of glacial times, a mere 2 million years on the geologic charts.

All birds belong to the class Aves (we are in the class Mammalia). Depending on the taxonomist, Aves breaks down into twenty-eight orders of which the passerines (Passeriformes) include about 60 percent of the 9,021 kinds of birds. In total numbers, they comprise the most numerous birds on earth. Passerines vary in size from four-inch-long kinglets to twenty-six-inch-long ravens.

Passerines, also known as perching birds, have four toes, three directed forward and one backward; all toes join the foot at the same level. While many birds can easily sit and nest in trees (even gulls can perch), passerines are the masters of scrambling, hopping, flitting, and flying through mazes of branches, thorns, and tangles. At night, as birds hunker down in their roosts, tendons stretch down the legs into their toes, unconsciously gripping their perches as they sleep. If the sleeping bird teeters backward, the leg tendons lock on tighter. Passerines contain two groups, the oscines and suboscines. Oscines (songbirds) include 60 of the world's 174 bird families. There are 17 suboscine families (mostly tropical), but only the flycatchers occur widely in the United States and Canada. These include common birds such as phoebes, kingbirds, and peewees.

Suboscines have simple, instinctive calls with little variety; oscines learn much of their song from parents and neighbors. Nearly all of the world's great songsters, such as thrushes, wrens, and mockingbirds, are oscines.

Usually, male passerines do most of the singing to defend the territory from intruders, while females build the nest and incubate eggs. In some species, however, both sexes have well-developed voice boxes (syrinxes) and share responsibilities for defending the territories. For example, male and female northern orioles each have distinct songs which function to discourage other orioles of the same sex from entering their territory.

When the eggs of suboscines such as flycatchers are incubated, hatched, and reared in isolated rooms, the young at maturity call just like their parents. Similar experiments with bluebirds and other oscines have demonstrated that young birds in this group need to hear the songs of their parents during a sensitive window of time so that they can develop the usual song.

When populations of the same species become isolated, some species develop distinct regional dialects. When separated over large areas, dialects may become so different that birds can no longer recognize members of their species. For example, playback of cardinal calls from Texas elicited little response when played within the territories of Ontario cardinals.

Mockingbirds are well-known for their ability to learn new songs as evidenced by one talented bird who faithfully imitated the calls of fifty-five species in one hour. Some individual brown thrashers, relatives of mockingbirds, have an even greater repertoire of more than 2,000 different songs!

Birds with varied songs obtain certain advantages. Females listen longer to varied songs than to simpler songs, and varied singing repels intruders from the territory better than less complex songs. Complexity of the song may indicate the age and experience of the breeder and rivals are less likely to challenge older males that might prove to be better fighters. Likewise, some female songbirds may use song to pick experienced mates that might have better territories with more food for their young.

December 1995

DECEMBER

S	M	T	W	T	F	S
					1	2
3	4	5	6	7	8	9
10	11	12	13	14	15	16
17	18	19	20	21	22	23
24/31	25	26	27	28	29	30

4 MONDAY

5 TUESDAY

6 WEDNESDAY — Full Moon ○

7 THURSDAY

8 FRIDAY

9 SATURDAY

10 SUNDAY

Male northern oriole (*Icterus galbula*) on trumpet creeper (*Campsis radicans*). Duanesburg, New York. Nikon 8008S with 600mm lens, Kodachrome 64 at 1/60 second/F11. By J. Michael Fuller.

December 1995

DECEMBER						
S	M	T	W	T	F	S
					1	2
3	4	5	6	7	8	9
10	11	12	13	14	15	16
17	18	19	20	21	22	23
24/31	25	26	27	28	29	30

11 MONDAY

12 TUESDAY

13 WEDNESDAY

14 THURSDAY

15 FRIDAY

Last Quarter

16 SATURDAY

17 SUNDAY

Chanukah   MONDAY *18*

                                                    TUESDAY *19*

                                               WEDNESDAY *20*

New Moon   THURSDAY *21*
●

Solstice   FRIDAY *22*

                                                 SATURDAY *23*

                                                   SUNDAY *24*

December 1995

DECEMBER

S	M	T	W	T	F	S
					1	2
3	4	5	6	7	8	9
10	11	12	13	14	15	16
17	18	19	20	21	22	23
24/31	25	26	27	28	29	30

25 MONDAY   Christmas

26 TUESDAY   Boxing Day (Canada)

27 WEDNESDAY

28 THURSDAY   First Quarter
                                                ◑

29 FRIDAY

30 SATURDAY

31 SUNDAY

Mountain bluebird (*Sialia currucoides*) and bitter brush (*Funshia tridentata*). Lava Beds National Monument, California. Nikon FE2 with 400mm lens and teleconverter, Fujichrome RD 100 at 1/60 second/F11. By J. C. Miller.

January 1996

JANUARY

S	M	T	W	T	F	S
	1	2	3	4	5	6
7	8	9	10	11	12	13
14	15	16	17	18	19	20
21	22	23	24	25	26	27
28	29	30	31			

1 MONDAY   New Year's Day

2 TUESDAY

3 WEDNESDAY

4 THURSDAY

5 FRIDAY   Full Moon
                                             ◯

6 SATURDAY

7 SUNDAY

Brown thrasher (*Toxostoma rufum*) on staghorn sumac (*Rhus typhina*). West End Boat Basin, Jones Beach State Park, New York. Canon T90 with 500mm lens, Fujichrome 100 at 1/250 second/F8. By Harold and Kathy Lindstrom.

1994

JANUARY						
S	M	T	W	T	F	S
						1
2	3	4	5	6	7	8
9	10	11	12	13	14	15
16	17	18	19	20	21	22
23	24	25	26	27	28	29
30	31					

FEBRUARY						
S	M	T	W	T	F	S
		1	2	3	4	5
6	7	8	9	10	11	12
13	14	15	16	17	18	19
20	21	22	23	24	25	26
27	28					

MARCH						
S	M	T	W	T	F	S
		1	2	3	4	5
6	7	8	9	10	11	12
13	14	15	16	17	18	19
20	21	22	23	24	25	26
27	28	29	30	31		

APRIL						
S	M	T	W	T	F	S
					1	2
3	4	5	6	7	8	9
10	11	12	13	14	15	16
17	18	19	20	21	22	23
24	25	26	27	28	29	30

MAY						
S	M	T	W	T	F	S
1	2	3	4	5	6	7
8	9	10	11	12	13	14
15	16	17	18	19	20	21
22	23	24	25	26	27	28
29	30	31				

JUNE						
S	M	T	W	T	F	S
			1	2	3	4
5	6	7	8	9	10	11
12	13	14	15	16	17	18
19	20	21	22	23	24	25
26	27	28	29	30		

JULY						
S	M	T	W	T	F	S
					1	2
3	4	5	6	7	8	9
10	11	12	13	14	15	16
17	18	19	20	21	22	23
24	25	26	27	28	29	30
31						

AUGUST						
S	M	T	W	T	F	S
	1	2	3	4	5	6
7	8	9	10	11	12	13
14	15	16	17	18	19	20
21	22	23	24	25	26	27
28	29	30	31			

SEPTEMBER						
S	M	T	W	T	F	S
				1	2	3
4	5	6	7	8	9	10
11	12	13	14	15	16	17
18	19	20	21	22	23	24
25	26	27	28	29	30	

OCTOBER						
S	M	T	W	T	F	S
						1
2	3	4	5	6	7	8
9	10	11	12	13	14	15
16	17	18	19	20	21	22
23	24	25	26	27	28	29
30	31					

NOVEMBER						
S	M	T	W	T	F	S
		1	2	3	4	5
6	7	8	9	10	11	12
13	14	15	16	17	18	19
20	21	22	23	24	25	26
27	28	29	30			

DECEMBER						
S	M	T	W	T	F	S
				1	2	3
4	5	6	7	8	9	10
11	12	13	14	15	16	17
18	19	20	21	22	23	24
25	26	27	28	29	30	31

1996

JANUARY						
S	M	T	W	T	F	S
	1	2	3	4	5	6
7	8	9	10	11	12	13
14	15	16	17	18	19	20
21	22	23	24	25	26	27
28	29	30	31			

FEBRUARY						
S	M	T	W	T	F	S
				1	2	3
4	5	6	7	8	9	10
11	12	13	14	15	16	17
18	19	20	21	22	23	24
25	26	27	28	29		

MARCH						
S	M	T	W	T	F	S
					1	2
3	4	5	6	7	8	9
10	11	12	13	14	15	16
17	18	19	20	21	22	23
24	25	26	27	28	29	30
31						

APRIL						
S	M	T	W	T	F	S
	1	2	3	4	5	6
7	8	9	10	11	12	13
14	15	16	17	18	19	20
21	22	23	24	25	26	27
28	29	30				

MAY						
S	M	T	W	T	F	S
			1	2	3	4
5	6	7	8	9	10	11
12	13	14	15	16	17	18
19	20	21	22	23	24	25
26	27	28	29	30	31	

JUNE						
S	M	T	W	T	F	S
						1
2	3	4	5	6	7	8
9	10	11	12	13	14	15
16	17	18	19	20	21	22
23	24	25	26	27	28	29
30						

JULY						
S	M	T	W	T	F	S
	1	2	3	4	5	6
7	8	9	10	11	12	13
14	15	16	17	18	19	20
21	22	23	24	25	26	27
28	29	30	31			

AUGUST						
S	M	T	W	T	F	S
				1	2	3
4	5	6	7	8	9	10
11	12	13	14	15	16	17
18	19	20	21	22	23	24
25	26	27	28	29	30	31

SEPTEMBER						
S	M	T	W	T	F	S
1	2	3	4	5	6	7
8	9	10	11	12	13	14
15	16	17	18	19	20	21
22	23	24	25	26	27	28
29	30					

OCTOBER						
S	M	T	W	T	F	S
		1	2	3	4	5
6	7	8	9	10	11	12
13	14	15	16	17	18	19
20	21	22	23	24	25	26
27	28	29	30	31		

NOVEMBER						
S	M	T	W	T	F	S
					1	2
3	4	5	6	7	8	9
10	11	12	13	14	15	16
17	18	19	20	21	22	23
24	25	26	27	28	29	30

DECEMBER						
S	M	T	W	T	F	S
1	2	3	4	5	6	7
8	9	10	11	12	13	14
15	16	17	18	19	20	21
22	23	24	25	26	27	28
29	30	31				

1995

JANUARY

S	M	T	W	T	F	S
1	2	3	4	5	6	7
8	9	10	11	12	13	14
15	16	17	18	19	20	21
22	23	24	25	26	27	28
29	30	31				

FEBRUARY

S	M	T	W	T	F	S
			1	2	3	4
5	6	7	8	9	10	11
12	13	14	15	16	17	18
19	20	21	22	23	24	25
26	27	28				

MARCH

S	M	T	W	T	F	S
			1	2	3	4
5	6	7	8	9	10	11
12	13	14	15	16	17	18
19	20	21	22	23	24	25
26	27	28	29	30	31	

APRIL

S	M	T	W	T	F	S
						1
2	3	4	5	6	7	8
9	10	11	12	13	14	15
16	17	18	19	20	21	22
23	24	25	26	27	28	29
30						

MAY

S	M	T	W	T	F	S
	1	2	3	4	5	6
7	8	9	10	11	12	13
14	15	16	17	18	19	20
21	22	23	24	25	26	27
28	29	30	31			

JUNE

S	M	T	W	T	F	S
				1	2	3
4	5	6	7	8	9	10
11	12	13	14	15	16	17
18	19	20	21	22	23	24
25	26	27	28	29	30	

JULY

S	M	T	W	T	F	S
						1
2	3	4	5	6	7	8
9	10	11	12	13	14	15
16	17	18	19	20	21	22
23	24	25	26	27	28	29
30	31					

AUGUST

S	M	T	W	T	F	S
		1	2	3	4	5
6	7	8	9	10	11	12
13	14	15	16	17	18	19
20	21	22	23	24	25	26
27	28	29	30	31		

SEPTEMBER

S	M	T	W	T	F	S
					1	2
3	4	5	6	7	8	9
10	11	12	13	14	15	16
17	18	19	20	21	22	23
24	25	26	27	28	29	30

OCTOBER

S	M	T	W	T	F	S
1	2	3	4	5	6	7
8	9	10	11	12	13	14
15	16	17	18	19	20	21
22	23	24	25	26	27	28
29	30	31				

NOVEMBER

S	M	T	W	T	F	S
			1	2	3	4
5	6	7	8	9	10	11
12	13	14	15	16	17	18
19	20	21	22	23	24	25
26	27	28	29	30		

DECEMBER

S	M	T	W	T	F	S
					1	2
3	4	5	6	7	8	9
10	11	12	13	14	15	16
17	18	19	20	21	22	23
24	25	26	27	28	29	30
31						

Birding Resources

The following lists offer a sample of available birding resources.

FIELD GUIDES

The Audubon Society Field Guide to North American Birds: Eastern Region, by John Bull and John Farrand, Jr. New York: Alfred A. Knopf, 1977.

The Audubon Society Field Guide to North American Birds: Western Region, by Miklos D. F. Udvardy. New York: Alfred A. Knopf, 1977.

The Audubon Society Master Guide to Birding, edited by John Farrand, Jr. 3 vols. New York: Alfred A. Knopf, 1983.

The Audubon Society Pocket Guides: Familiar Birds of North America, Eastern Region; Familiar Birds of North America, Western Region. Edited by Ann H. Whitman; Kenn Kaufman and John Farrand, Jr., consultants. New York: Alfred A. Knopf, 1986.

The Birder's Handbook, by Paul R. Ehrlich, David S. Dobkin, and Darryl Wheye. New York: Simon & Schuster, Inc., 1988.

The Birds Around Us, by Roger Tory Peterson. San Francisco: Ortho Books, 1986.

Birds of North America, revised edition, by Chandler S. Robbins, Bertel Bruun, and Herbert S. Zim. New York: Golden Press, 1983.

Field Guide to the Birds of North America, revised edition, by the National Geographic Society. Washington: National Geographic Society, 1987.

A Field Guide to Western Birds, by Roger Tory Peterson. Boston: Houghton Mifflin Co., 1990.

National Audubon Society Birdfeeder Handbook of North America, by Robert Burton. New York: Dorling Kindersley, 1992.

Roger Tory Peterson's Field Guide to Birds, 4th edition. Boston: Houghton Mifflin Co., 1980.

MAGAZINES

American Birds, 700 Broadway, New York, NY 10003

Audubon magazine, 700 Broadway, New York, NY 10003

Birding, American Birding Association, P.O. Box 31, Honeoye Falls, NY 14472

Bird Watchers Digest, P.O. Box 110, Marietta, OH 45750

Birder's World, 720 E. 8th St., Holland, MI 49423

Living Bird, Laboratory of Ornithology at Cornell University, 159 Sapsucker Woods Rd., Ithaca, NY 14850

Wild Bird, Fancy Publications, P.O. Box 6050, Mission Viejo, CA 92690

Wingtips, Box 226, Lansing, NY 14882

Videoguides

The Audubon Society Videoguides to Birds of North America, vols. 1–5, Godfrey-Stadin Productions. Distributed by MasterVision, New York, NY 10028

The National Audubon Society's UP CLOSE Videos: Bluebirds; Cardinals; Hawks; Hummingbirds; Owls; Nature Science Network, Carrboro, NC 27510

For a list of all Audubon bird-related publications and products write:

Licensing Department
National Audubon Society
700 Broadway
New York, NY 10003

The National Audubon Society

AT THE National Audubon Society,* our mission is to protect the wildlife and wildlife habitat upon which our lives depend. Together with more than 600,000 members and an extensive chapter network, our professional staff of scientists, lobbyists, lawyers, policy analysts, and educators is fighting to save threatened ecosystems and to restore the natural balance that is critical to the quality of life on our planet. Our underlying belief is that all forms of life are interdependent and that the diversity of nature is essential to both our economic and environmental well-being.

CHAPTERS

Audubon's 600,000 members provide the underpinning for all the society's programs and activities. Two-thirds of our members also belong to local Audubon chapters, now numbering more than 500, which serve in their communities as focal points for conservation, nature education, and citizen action on environmental issues.

SANCTUARIES

Audubon, through its nationwide system of sanctuaries, protects more than a quarter-million acres of essential habitat and unique natural areas for birds, other wild animals, and rare plant life. The sanctuaries range in size from twelve acres around Theodore Roosevelt's grave in New York State to twenty-six thousand acres of coastal marsh in Louisiana. Most of the sanctuaries are staffed by resident wardens who also patrol adjacent natural areas not owned by Audubon.

REGIONAL OFFICES

We also maintain regional and state offices staffed by full-time professional conservationists, who advance Audubon programs throughout the fifty states. Regional staff members guide and coordinate the

*National Audubon Society and Audubon are trademarks of the National Audubon Society, Inc.

varied activities of the many Audubon chapters, from operating nature centers to engaging in environmental litigation. They work on specific environmental issues and conduct leadership training workshops for citizen activists, to ensure the recruitment of a growing corps of citizen volunteers who are ready and able to participate effectively in the environmental policy process at every level of government.

GOVERNMENT RELATIONS

Through the staff of our Washington, D.C., office on Capitol Hill, Audubon maintains liaisons with federal agencies, testifies before Congress on legislative proposals related to our primary concerns, and pursues environmental litigation through court action to remedy threats to wildlife habitats. We also cooperate with other conservation organizations on local and national levels.

SCIENTIFIC ACTIVITIES

Our staff conducts wildlife research to help guide the restoration and management of natural areas including Audubon Sanctuaries and to aid in the recovery of endangered species such as wood storks and piping plovers. The work of these staff people is augmented by that of other scientists to ensure that our positions on such crucial environmental concerns as marine conservation, energy, global climate change, water management, solid waste, and population have a sound, rational basis. We employ consultants to review available data and to outline options on complex technical issues. We convene frequent conferences, workshops, and seminars to discuss and disseminate timely information on important environmental issues.

PUBLICATIONS

Our award-winning *Audubon* magazine, published six times a year, carries outstanding articles and color photography on wildlife and nature, and presents in-depth reports on critical environmental issues, as well as conservation news and comment. *Audubon* is sent to all members and, by subscription, to thousands of libraries, schools, and government agencies. Special members and supporters will also receive our monthly *Audubon Activist* newsjournal that keeps them up to date on environmental issues. We also publish *American Birds,* an ornithological journal that reports on the distribution, migration, and abundance of North American birds.

EDUCATION

Our educational staff provides information on environmental concerns in response to thousands of inquiries each month from our members and from the public. Through the educational activities of our chapters, thousands of young people are made aware of the natural world around them. We also operate education centers throughout the country. There, teacher-naturalists hold outdoor classes for schoolchildren and other groups, as well as provide outreach and teacher training at local schools and parks. Our summer ecology camps—in Maine, Connecticut, and Wyoming—provide intensive study sessions for adults and carry optional university credit. *Audubon Adventures,* a bimonthly four-page children's nature newspaper, reaches hundreds of thousands of elementary school students. The Audubon Expedition Institute offers travel-study programs in the United States for high school and college students.

TRAVEL

Audubon's travel program sponsors more than twenty-five exciting trips every year to exotic places like Alaska, Antarctica, Baja California, Galapagos, Great Britain, Indonesia, Japan, and Patagonia. All tour operators must comply with our *Travel Ethic for Environmentally Responsible Travel,* and each trip is led by an experienced Audubon senior staff member. Special discounts are available—contact the Travel Department for additional information.

TELEVISION

National Audubon Society Television Specials can be seen on TBS Superstations. Accompanying books and educational computer software give viewers an opportunity for further enjoyment of the subjects covered by the television series.

LICENSED PRODUCTS

Audubon also has many licensed products, which, when purchased, help fund the programs mentioned above. These items include our award-winning calendars, holiday greeting cards, oversized books, field guides, videoguides, porcelain figurines, binoculars, birdseed, bird feeders, stained glass, philatelics, VISA affinity credit card, personal checks, T-shirts, jigsaw puzzles, and nature recordings.

For more information about Audubon, write or call us at:
National Audubon Society
700 Broadway
New York, New York 10003
(212) 979-3000

NATIONAL AUDUBON SOCIETY HEADQUARTERS AND
REGIONAL AND STATE OFFICES

National Headquarters
700 Broadway
New York, New York 10003
(212) 979-3000

Capital Office/Government Relations
666 Pennsylvania Avenue, SE
Washington, DC 20003
(202) 547-9009

Alaska Regional Office
308 G Street, Room 217
Anchorage, Alaska 99501
(907) 276-7034

Great Lakes Regional Office
(Illinois, Indiana, Kentucky, Michigan,
    Minnesota, Ohio, Wisconsin)
692 North High Street
Suite 208
Columbus, Ohio 43215
(614) 224-3303

Hawaii State Office
212 Merchant St., Suite 320
Honolulu, Hawaii 96813
(808) 522-5566

Maine State Office
P.O. Box 524
Dover-Foxcroft, Maine 04426
(207) 564-7946

Mid-Atlantic Regional Office
(Delaware, District of Columbia,
    Maryland, New Jersey, Pennsylvania,
    Virginia, West Virginia)
1104 Fernwood Avenue, Suite 300
Camp Hill, Pennsylvania 17011
(717) 763-4985

Minnesota State Office and
    Audubon Council
26 East Exchange Street
Suite 207
St. Paul, Minnesota 55101
(612) 225-1830

New Mexico State Office
Randall Davey Audubon Center
P.O. Box 9314
Santa Fe, New Mexico 87504
(505) 983-4609

Northeast Regional Office
(Connecticut, Maine, Massachusetts,
    New Hampshire, New York, Rhode
    Island, Vermont)
1789 Western Avenue
Albany, New York 12203
(518) 869-9731

Rocky Mountain Regional Office
(Arizona, Colorado, Idaho, Montana,
    Utah, Wyoming)
4150 Darley Avenue, Suite 5
Boulder, Colorado 80303
(303) 499-0223/0219

Southeast Regional Office
(Alabama, Florida, Georgia, Mississippi,
    North Carolina, Puerto Rico, South
    Carolina, Tennessee)
102 East Fourth Avenue
Tallahassee, Florida 32303
(904) 222-2473

Southwest Regional Office
(Louisiana, Guatemala, Mexico, New
    Mexico, Panama, Texas)
2525 Wallingwood, Suite 301
Austin, Texas 78746
(512) 327-1943/1946

Vermont State Office
Fiddler's Green, Box 9
Waitsfield, Vermont 05673
(802) 496-5727

West Central Regional Office
(Arkansas, Iowa, Kansas, Missouri,
  Nebraska, North Dakota, Oklahoma,
  South Dakota)
200 South Wind Place, Suite 205
Manhattan, Kansas 66502
(913) 537-4385

Washington State Office
P.O. Box 462
Olympia, Washington 98507
(206) 786-8020

Western Regional Office
(California, Guam, Hawaii, Nevada,
  Oregon, Washington)
555 Audubon Place
Sacramento, California 95825
(916) 481-5332

EDUCATION CENTERS AND OFFICES

National Education Office
  Department Headquarters
700 Broadway
New York, New York 10003
(212) 979-3000

National Center for Environmental
  Education
Audubon Center in Greenwich
613 Riversville Road
Greenwich, Connecticut 06831
(203) 869-5272

Audubon Center of the Northwoods
Route 1
Sandstone, Minnesota 55072
(612) 245-2648

Audubon Expedition Institute
P.O. Box 365
Belfast, Maine 04915
(207) 338-5859

Aullwood Audubon Center and Farm
1000 Aullwood Road
Dayton, Ohio 45414
(513) 890-7360

National Audubon Society
Los Angeles Education Office
200 Culver Boulevard
Playa del Rey, California 90293
(310) 574-2799

Northeast Audubon Center
Route 4, Box 171
Sharon, Connecticut 06069
(203) 364-0520

Randall Davey Audubon Center
P.O. Box 9314
Sante Fe, New Mexico 87504
(505) 983-4609

Richardson Bay Audubon Center
376 Greenwood Beach Road
Tiburon, California 94920
(415) 388-2524

Schlitz Audubon Center
1111 East Brown Deer Road
Milwaukee, Wisconsin 53217
(414) 352-2880

WILDLIFE SANCTUARIES

National Audubon Society
  Sanctuary Department Headquarters
93 West Cornwall Road
Sharon, Connecticut 06069
(203) 364-0048

Francis Beidler Forest Sanctuary
336 Sanctuary Road
Harleyville, South Carolina 29448
(803) 462-2150

Borestone Mountain Sanctuary
Box 112
Monson, Maine 04464
(207) 997-3607 (summer)
(207) 997-3558 (winter)

Clyde E. Buckley Sanctuary
1305 Germany Road
Frankfort, Kentucky 40601
(606) 873-5711

Constitution Marsh Sanctuary
RFD #2, Route 9D
Garrison, New York 10524
(914) 265-2601

Corkscrew Swamp Sanctuary
375 Sanctuary Road
Naples, Florida 33964
(813) 657-3771/4662

Dauphin Island Sanctuary
P.O. Box 369-370
Dauphin Island, Alabama 36528
(205) 861-2141

Richardson Bay Audubon Center
   and Sanctuary
376 Greenwood Beach Road
Tiburon, California 94920
(415) 388-2524

Theodore Roosevelt Sanctuary
134 Cove Road
Oyster Bay, New York 11771
(516) 922-3200

Sabal Palm Grove
P.O. Box 5052
Brownsville, Texas 78523
(512) 541-8034

SCIENCE AND FIELD RESEARCH OFFICES

Science Division Department
   Headquarters
700 Broadway
New York, New York 10003
(212) 979-3000

Corkscrew Science Center
479 Sanctuary Road
Naples, Florida 33964
(813) 657-2531

Scully Science Center
550 South Bay Avenue
Islip, New York 11751
(516) 224-3669

Seabird Restoration Program
   and Project Puffin
159 Sapsucker Woods Road
Ithaca, New York 14850
(607) 257-7308 (winter)
(207) 529-5828 (summer)

Membership in the National Audubon Society will bring you . . .

- One year (six bimonthly issues) of award-winning *Audubon* magazine.
- Membership in your local Audubon chapter and participation in its exciting programs and special events.
- The opportunity to visit Audubon Nature Centers and Sanctuaries and to attend Audubon Ecology Camps and Workshops.
- The chance to receive our free monthly newsletter, the *Audubon Activist.*
- Eligibility for travel discounts.
- Special offers on nature books, gifts, and collectibles.
- The satisfaction of knowing that your membership helps support sanctuaries, field research, environmental education, environmental legislation, and other efforts critical to the protection of wildlife and the environment.

MEMBERSHIP APPLICATION

Yes, I want to join the
NATIONAL AUDUBON SOCIETY

Enroll me as a member, start my subscription to *Audubon,* and send me my membership card, which entitles me to all the benefits and privileges of National Audubon Society membership.

Please make check payable to National Audubon Society and mail to Membership Data Center, P.O. Box 52529, Boulder, Colorado 80322-2529. The special introductory rate is $20. I save $15!

☐ Check enclosed ☐ Please bill me

Name _____

Address _____

City _____ State _____ Zip _____

5ET43